ALEX MAZEY
Living in Disneyland

I0163033

BROKEN SLEEP BOOKS

Published 2020,
Broken Sleep Books:
Cornwall / Wales

brokensleepbooks.com

First Edition

Lay out your unrest.

Publisher/Editor: Aaron Kent
Editor: Charlie Baylis

Typeset in UK by Aaron Kent

Broken Sleep Books is committed to
a sustainable future for our planet,
and therefore uses print on
demand publication.

brokensleepbooks@gmail.com

ISBN: 9798608584053

'They are spirits of demons performing miraculous signs...'
Revelation 16:13

'We're all living in Amerika...'
Rammstein

Contents

Living in Disneyland

Alex Mazey

Are we Living in Disneyland?

A shallow interpretation of our consumerism today maintains that we are all given an 'illusion of choice'. *Coca-Cola* is Republican, and *Pepsi* is Democrat, with this key conceptualisation of politics as soft drinks pertaining that either choice is bad for you. However, it's precisely that choice of substituting one product for another that, in turn, develops our identity from the culture of significance that holds us captive. These choices are not academic or theoretical, but rather represent the day to day, unconscious desires of our ego, pertaining to how we would like to be represented to the outside world. In short, we find representation in our commodities because of this very reliance on sign-value.

What if I said *Perrier's Citron Lemon-Lime* and Perrier's *Pamplemousse Rose* both exist to supplement the illusion of *Perrier Natural*, similar to how *This Juicy Water* exists to imply *Evian Water* as a healthy, natural alternative? Of course, no choice is authentically natural, here – or healthy – but rather each a 'product' or 'commodity' with its own ideological significance. While it is commonly accepted that new commodities are continuously introduced to the market to offer more choice, hyperreality actually suggests that new products exist to sustain the illusion of a company's flagship commodity, which when viewed in isolation would become another nonsensical abstraction.

These choices are extended to our aesthetic tastes, which have become increasingly absorbed by this system of signs, as laid out by Jean Baudrillard in '*The System of Objects*'. This is what makes consumerism so alluring to us; it is not just a world of cheap illusions where the masses have been duped by some monstrous corporation, but rather an appeal to our base instincts, our selfish desires for some narcissistic gratification. In many ways, these techniques attempt to fulfil a spiritual emptiness.

In '*American Psycho*', when Patrick Bateman demonstrates his inner resentment at his colleague's superior business card, he knows he has been out-done by a 'tasteful thickness' – crushingly defeated – in this game of signs and signifiers, especially in regards to his own failed representation as the most powerful man in the room. In many ways, we all operate like Patrick Bateman looking to compete with our neighbours over the picket fences of our own egos. The power of our system lies in how it promotes not only the material successes of the uncompromising capitalist but also the moral virtue of the revolutionary activist.

Do we really believe that the same companies that led to ecological devastation – and historical oppression of the wage-earner – suddenly care about educated children and deforestation? In reality, there is no 'they care' but rather 'we care'. In the modern world, advertisement understands the importance of customer satisfaction, and there's nothing more economically satisfying than peddling the moral virtue that helps a consumer sleep at night. And so, consumers buy *Ben & Jerry's ice cream*, not to fuel an addiction to sugar, but rather to relive the victories of emancipation. This progressive idea of a separation between the conscious and unconscious consumer is yet another fiction in the game of hyperreality.

Perhaps, a more thematically relevant example of our unconscious states of hyperreality could be taken from a film like Gore Verbinski's *'A Cure for Wellness'*. Despite becoming a hugely unsuccessful, box-office failure, this psychological horror shows us the pervasive effects of nefarious illusions, negated only by a protagonist increasing his conscious state to one of heightened awareness. From the outset, the film follows the journey of a young business executive as he travels to a hydropathy clinic located in the atmospheric gothique of the Swiss Alps. Emblematic of the youthful, precarious accomplishments of a vague capitalist America, our troubled protagonist, Lockhart, is tasked with bringing home an increasingly estranged CEO, Roland Pembroke; who must face the criminal charges of corporate misconduct.

We observe Lockhart leaving the tangible, materialist world of financial services before ascending towards the mysterious, phantasmagorical realms of Dr Heinreich Volmer's 'wellness centre', where patients drink spring water imbued with a miraculously restorative property. Unable to locate Pembroke at the clinic, Lockhart is told by a mysterious girl that 'nobody ever leaves' and an accident later renders him to the status of 'patient'. Here, Lockhart begins his journey of mental deliquescence, increasingly unable to distinguish what's real and what isn't.

Of course, unlike the passive viewership, Lockhart soon discovers the dark truth of his own world; that is, despite ingesting large quantities of the spring water, the patients are suffering from profound dehydration. What was promised as a cure to the ailments of the modern world, actually exasperated the issues of his own 'depleted immune system', whereby all patients were made increasingly sick under the pretence of a cure. What's more, the water is distilled through the patients to produce a life-giving essence, that vastly extends the natural lives of Dr Heinreich Volmer, his staff, and the mysterious girl, Hannah, whom Lockhart gradually befriends through some awkward romantic interaction.

Similar to this fiction, the system of signs is sustained by the distillation process of consumption, an essence that grows stronger through each generational proliferation – an everlasting quintessence. (It is no coincidence that the evil, manipulative characters' lives in 'A Cure for Wellness' are unnaturally sustained through the sweat and willing ignorance of their victims.) Isn't this exactly how a neoliberal, capitalist realism works? The pervasive, technocratic advances of the future presented to us as tangible solutions, despite bringing a level of fatal, life-draining suffering and environmental degradation; a profundity sustained by our blind acceptance of a universal framework; a diagnosis we didn't need – our cure for wellness.

Following the defeat of Dr Volmer, the wellness clinic is burnt to the ground through the illuminating grandeur of arson. The surviving patients look on at the wreckage with the warped, existential angst of a fallen system. Meanwhile, Lockhart returns to a secondary, global world of illusion; that is, into the remnants of the hyperreal dystopia from which he came. Hannah clutches to him on the back of a bike, representing not only her freedom but perhaps her saviour's newfound perspective, a clarity beyond nihilism. And while Lockhart has rescued Hannah from her own perverse, corrupt, illusionary world, we wonder if Hannah will rescue Lockhart from his. The real story of a fiery revolution begins here, in the manic face of a corporate lackey.

Miguel F. Doria at the Centre for Environmental Risk at the University of East Anglia, produced a white paper in 2006, titled *'Bottled water versus tap water: understanding consumers' preferences.'* According to Doria's research, 'a relatively large proportion of bottled water (between 40–60% globally) consists of packaged tap water[.]' Unsurprisingly enough, Doria's research revealed that 'from a strictly objective perspective, bottled water is not necessarily "better" or "worse" than tap water[…]' despite a schism in 'the media and scientific literature' regarding 'the merits and faults of each alternative.' While Doria's research provides a good overview of the general scientism, the paper reads with a subtle disingenuity, especially in regards to explaining the diverse possibilities 'for the increase of bottled water consumption.' According to his research, organoleptic reasons – the poor taste of tap water – was often given as an example of why people preferred bottled water. This is fascinating as it indicates the general milieu of the consumerist culture looking for satisfaction in everything, including the vital hydration of their bodies. The maintenance of one's health and wellbeing are almost used continuously as an opportunity for some cursory gratification. It seems the consumer will always view tap water in relation to the sugary delights of an ice-cold, *Coca-Cola.* This is an ideal representation of the Baudrillardian system of signs at work. Moreover, we can extend this analysis to other areas of our lives.

All breakfast cereals are competing with the appeal of an extra twenty minutes in bed; hence the proliferation of a market based on high-sugar products that appeal to both convenience and 'great taste', whilst also promoting a dialectic of natural authenticity. The task of preparing early morning sustenance is often presented as a task of dissatisfaction as if gratification should be the object of all our daily endeavours.

This warped, consumerist mentally is almost always present in advertisements and marketing; for example, where gyms promote vanity and personal aesthetics, over health and well-being. (Interestingly enough, even contraception promotes sensation over safety.)

Even so, a great deal of marketing offers to share in this illusion of health and wellbeing by externalising the abstraction to the abstract lives of other people. When we visit the supermarket, we will buy coffee regardless, feeding unhealthy yet necessary and urgent addictions to stimulants and sugar. Despite this horror, we can, at the very least, share in the warm fuzzies felt by the beneficiaries of fair trade, forest regrowth, etc. It seems coffee companies are now more than happy to present the illusion of opportunity and wellbeing for the future of its wage-earners. Of course, this is all done to conceal a purchase based on our own, shallow gratification.

Many consumers would like to believe this doesn't apply to them. They'd say, 'if coffee suppliers weren't ethical, I simply wouldn't buy the coffee'. If this is you, ask yourself, why doesn't this ethical virtue ever extend to the technology in your pocket or the clothes on your back? Along these lines, I suspect we will soon see the emergence of 'Ethical Technologies'; phones made by smiling faces, rather than, say, the child-slaves of the present day. This isn't a particularly revolutionary insight but rather another opportunity to point out how an abstract product; that is, coffee itself, absorbs yet another layer of abstraction, augmenting its chain of sign-value significance beyond mere societal prestige, elevating itself, ergo the consumer, with an additional sense of moral virtue.

On a Highstreet of cellophane sandwiches, soymilk lattes and pseudo-healthy choices, *Burger King* becomes a revolutionary experience of pure ideological desire. Here, products that are sold as health foods elsewhere are sold with a true-faced manifestation of their genuine depravity. The vegan activists campaigning outside offer an alternative vision that seems perhaps even more alienating and post-material than the industrial-scale, brutal slaughter of animals. This conceals the animus of veganism as perhaps another heightened sense of moral virtue against the masses; after all, what's saving animals against the spiritually fulfilling melodrama of resentment? Even so, Highstreet activism gets two things right: the comfort of crotch drops and analysis of legality as a product of power.

Ironically, healthy alternatives are almost always accompanied by *Coca-Cola*. A drink hardly ever criticised, but rather where cutting analysis is outsourced to the means by which the liquid is transmitted from can to mouth. I imagine the controversy surrounding plastic straws is almost entirely an attempt to avoid the criticism of the products themselves.

Philip K. Dick provides a vital conclusion, here: "Fake realities will create fake humans. Or, fake humans will generate fake realities and then sell them to other humans, turning them, eventually, into forgeries of themselves. So, we wind up with fake humans inventing fake realities and then peddling them to other fake humans. It is just a gigantic version of Disneyland."

Say It with Me

Reward cards. Advances in technology. Easy living.
Happy hour. Two for one. One for two. Gift wrapped.
Restoring meaning to your life with a positive outlook.

Restoring vitality with a gym membership. Eating in
moderation. Drinking responsibly. Treating yourself.
Living in the fast lane. Taking it easy. No regrets.

A strong economy. A diverse and low-risk society.
Money for the poor. Affordable healthcare. Good food
and good morals. Shopping in megamalls. Lipstick –

in different shades. Coffee grown on the mountainside.
Happy farmers with educated children. All paper cups
fighting deforestation. Obvious without complexity.

All the answers. No explanation needed. No need
to worry. New flavours available. Collect all colours.

Seizing the Memes of Production

A disembodied head stares towards a plastic water bottle. The text observes, 'Ah, yes. Enslaved moisture.' This is a representation of millennial humour characterised by states of both nihilism and absurdity. Offering another example, Elizabeth Bruenig of the *Washington Post* writes, 'The wiener is not a socialist icon; in fact, he is a breakdancing sausage from a Snapchat filter. His inclusion in a lineup of the U.S.S.R.'s patron saints doesn't mean anything.'

She writes that memes are about spending 'time in a dream world', an insight that ignores the dream world of our waking lives. She writes 'nothing coherent is left' while forgetting the coherency of the things we have displayed to us. The absurdist element of Bruenig's writing is when she uses adjectives like 'jolly' to appeal to an ageing demographic of *Washington Post* readers, who cannot be seen to understand the poignancy of memes; the disembodied heads staring towards plastic water bottles; the critical powers of the conscious mind.

Elizabeth Bruenig recounts the time she spoke to Adam Downer about 'the strangest meme he ever worked on': 'The meme consists of four panels, the first including the phrase "Hey Beter," a riff on "Hey Peter," referring to the main character of the comedy cartoon series "Family Guy." What comes next seems to make even less sense: In one iteration, the Sesame Street character Elmo (wearing a "suck my a–" T-shirt) calls out to Peter, then asks him to spell "whomst've," then blasts him with blue lasers. In the final panel, readers are advised to "follow for a free *iPhone 5*." (There is no prize.)

"That one was inexplicably popular," Downer told me. "I think it got popular because it was this giant emptiness of meaning. It was this giant race to the bottom of irony."'

What strikes me about this analysis is the inability to observe the obvious criticism of our relentless desire for products – and perhaps more strikingly – the people who manipulate that desire for their own nefarious purposes. We do not know who to 'follow' for a free iPhone 5 – and we know there is 'no prize.' What really matters is the product as elevated to the level of desire – everything else is meaningless; an intertextual narrative operating as a means to an end. Indicative types like Elizabeth Bruenig and Adam Downer are guilty of an unseen admission that states 'memes are meaningless because I am unable to comprehend them.'

So, what is a breakdancing sausage from a *Snapchat* filter doing in a lineup of Karl Marx, Friedrich Engels, Vladimir Lenin, and Joseph Stalin? Here, I can offer a two-pronged interpretation. On one side of the coin, the breakdancing sausage is emblematic of the empty, vapid culture of late-stage capitalism. It becomes a co-opted figure of rebellion. In the age of anonymity and avatars, the breakdancing sausage is the new socialist icon – because you wouldn't expect the face of a politician, would you? Our second interpretation becomes increasingly desolate and bleak, with Bruenig's wiener operating not a socialist icon, but as a symbolic figure of the failures of communism as associated with the rise of an Authoritarian-Left. The neoliberal, fascist, consumer-driven, weak-socialism of the West becomes embodied by a breakdancing sausage. Why breakdancing? In his 1986 book, *'America'*, Jean Baudrillard writes:

"Breakdancing is a feat of acrobatic gymnastics. Only at the end do you realise it actually was dancing, when the dancer freezes into a lazy, languid pose (elbow on the ground, head nonchalantly resting in the palm of the hand, the pose you see on Etruscan tombs). […] You might say that in curling up and spiralling around on the ground like this, they seem to be digging a hole for themselves within their own bodies, from which to stare out in the ironic, indolent pose of the dead."

Breakdancing offers a vision of a dying world, caught up in the ecstasy of acceleration. And while our products and software continue down channels that propound ease of comprehension, memes operate as another reaction to the reduction of human complexity, where nuance and discussion are stripped of their meaningful contributions. People attack complexity when they are incapable of it – our societies reward the obvious. Elevating simplicity implies simplicity. When our attitudes and institutions are so bereft of complexity, our brains become hardwired to dismiss and detract when faced with complication or inconsistency.

A disembodied head stares towards a plastic water bottle. The text observes, 'Ah, yes. Enslaved moisture.' Why, though? In many ways, we all operate as disembodied, formless heads. Whether we are meme-ing from the comfort of our beds, or working from the confinement of office cubicles, our minds occupy digital spaces. Our bodies become deliquescent, then our minds. We have become enslaved moisture. The residue of a thousand disembodied voices.

Ah, yes, Enslaved Moisture

It's 2013. A trained team of men and women explore a mine lost to the darkness of subterranean Canada. Above them, on the surface of the modern world, the shivering trees of Ontario stand with the fresh lushness of fallen rain. Below the surface, these curious scientists are not prospecting for rich veins of metal ore, but perhaps something far more precious; that is, the water that has seeped freely through the earth for millennia. Ontario's border with the United States follows the inland waterways eastwards, up towards the Saint Lawrence River drainage system, where fresh water meets the crashing waves of the Atlantic Ocean; a sea that separates the old world from the new. It should come as no surprise then, when I say Ontario is home to the oldest recorded pocket of water, found by those same scientists back in 2013. A pocket of water recorded as 2.6 billion years old.

Designed to access liquid resources like water, wells are one of the earliest recorded human inventions. Early designs were hand dug through the dusty wastelands of dry sedimentation, with later arrangements constructed in increasingly ingenious forms, like that of the qanat and aqueduct. In 2009, archaeologists from Edinburgh University discovered wells near the coastal town of Paphos, Cyprus. Inhabited since the Neolithic period, Paphos is recorded on the UNESCO list of cultural and natural treasures of the world's heritage, with its stone-age wells radiocarbon dated to approximately 10,500 years ago. The settlement of Paphos was built on a hill that looked out towards the blue, rolling Mediterranean, with a few miles of fertile soil so beautiful it became the birthplace of Aphrodite, where the goddess of love rose from the sea.

Charting a course through the Ionian and Adriatic, we might reach Central Europe, the Greater Leipzig region where we find evidence of water wells as the oldest timber constructions in the world. Through the use of dendrochronology, scientists are able to estimate the exact felling years of the trees used by early Neolithic settlers. These ancient water wells operated as a catalyst of civilization, paving the way for irrigation and agriculture; the assurance of permanent housing and the ongoing development of new skills like carpentry. This sequence of events is known, generally speaking, as the Neolithic Demographic Transition, where increasingly larger populations became possible.

As populations grew, issues of societies providing adequate sanitation arose, especially where the contamination of fresh drinking water was concerned. Whilst the Mayan civilization was initially well adapted to provide both food and water for its citizens, there is good evidence to suggest its downfall came with an inability to deal with the issues associated with rapid population growth; that is, primarily, concerns regarding waste management, contamination and disease.

The outbreak of cholera that occurred in 1854 near Broad Street in the Soho district of the City of Westminster, London, England, is another good example of how water supplies and their subsequent contamination by way of increasing amounts of human waste, can lead to the death and decay of entire populations when left untreated. It is widely believed that John Snow's study of the Broad Street water well and his hypothesis that germ-contaminated water conveyed infectious disease became a ground-breaking event that changed the way societies viewed sanitation and its effects on safe, drinking water.

It is usually argued that John Snow's miraculous study, alongside the philanthropic actions of a few powerful men, inevitably led to changes in water sanitation, when it was more likely the increasing absenteeism of the impoverished, disease-ridden, working-class, wage laborers that shook the government into action. A serious criticism of the South London water companies to act on issues of squalidity and sanitation is usually absent from the broader conversation, especially when it comes to public education. Why? Because over one-hundred years later, large-scale companies providing the services of global necessity still operate with a similar impunity.

The two water companies operating at the time of the cholera epidemic of 1854 were *Southwark Water Company*, and *Vauxhall Water Company*, both pumping water from the filth of the River Thames. A microbiologist of the time described their water as 'the most disgusting which I have ever examined'. Less than a year after another outbreak of the disease, both companies amalgamated to form a monopoly in the area, conveniently avoiding any potential scapegoating and repercussion from members of the now defunct Board of Health, whose administrative reforms for an improved public health had become increasingly unpopular with the laissez-faire capitalists of London's wealthy bourgeoisie.

An overview on *'Public Health Then and Now'* for the *'American Journal of Public Health'* produced by Nigel Paneth, MD, MPH, Peter Vinten-Johansen, PhD, Howard Brody, MD, PhD, and Michael Rip, PhD, titled, *'A Rivalry of Foulness: Official and Unofficial Investigations of the London Cholera*

Epidemic of 1854' states how, 'In spite of its limited powers, the Board of Health investigated many local sanitary deficiencies between 1848 and 1854 and issued several reports that aroused anxiety and irritation among business and medical interests. [...] As a result, on July 31, 1854, Parliament refused to renew the Board and dismissed its members, thus abolishing the only central public health body in the country just as England's third cholera epidemic of the century was getting under way.' The overview offers a detailed analysis of John Snow's science and the 'Implications for Contemporary Epidemiology' but offers very little response regarding the significance or impact on London's water wells. In fact, *Southwark and Vauxhall Waterworks Company* continued to pump filthy water right through to the 20th century, until the Metropolitan Water Board took over in 1904.

London's waterworks saw some tangible improvements under this single, publicly-owned body. The Metropolitan Water Board saw the foundation of the Metropolitan Water Board Employees' Association. This trade union consisted of water works' employees who successfully campaigned for a pay increase in 1923, increasing the living standards of its wage-earners. However, these accomplishments were short lived. In the same year Britain joined the European Union, the Metropolitan Water Board was largely reorganised by a parliamentary act, allowing the publicly-owned waterworks to pass to the Thames Water Authority. This authority later formed a monopoly over both water and waste management, operating as the private utility company, *Thames Water Utilities Ltd.*

On the 22nd March 2017, *The Guardian* reported that *Thames Water* had 'been hit with a record fine of £20.3m after huge leaks of untreated sewage into the Thames and its tributaries...' resulting in the death of surrounding wildlife. The Environment Agency described these sewage leaks as 'the biggest freshwater pollution case it had ever undertaken...' with the chief prosecutor criticising the company for 'the parlous state of its works.' Bearing in mind, *Thames Water*'s operating profit came in at £742m from a one-year period from between 2015 – 2016. *The Guardian* concluded that whilst these water companies continue to make huge profits, they actually pay 'little or no corporation tax'. From the present day, (and in Britain, especially,) these destructive companies now operate with a perverse monopoly over one of the genuine necessities of human life; that is, the naturally occurring liquid human beings actually need to survive.

In hindsight, the 1850's were an interesting time for water production. Whilst poor-quality drinking water exacerbated the cholera epidemics bared by impoverished communities throughout Britain, the *Schweppes* beverage company had begun its production of revolutionary, bottled drinking water.

Spring water from the range of Malvern Hills permeates through the fissures of hard granite rock, producing a flow rate of gallons of water per minute. Information provided by the Worcestershire County Council, suggests 1622 as 'the first record of spring water ever being bottled in the UK', taking place at the springs of 'Holy Well which later became the site where *Malvern Water* was first drawn for sale by the *Schweppes* Company at the Great Exhibition of 1851.' *The Medical Times and Gazette, Volume 12*, records an advertisement for the 'Schweppes Malvern Seltzer Water' of 1856:

This advertisement contains an acknowledgment of bottled water as pure artifice; 'artificial water' as an 'imitation of the natural spring.' Interestingly enough, this acknowledgement of bottled water's artifice and consequential imitative qualities are all but absent from today's promotional, beverage marketing. In fact, beverages such as the *Coca-Cola*-owned *This Juicy Water* now exist to imply their *Evian Water* as the genuine and authentic 'natural choice' when in fact – neither choice is natural – but rather each a 'product' with its own ideological attribution. Our blind subservience to this reality is now sustained by a serious inability to distinguish what's real from what isn't.

It's well recorded that *Schweppes* entered into a contract with the Ballard family in 1890, who began to supply the company with spring water as early as 1892, when a bottling factory was built on the village premises. Using local materials, the factory was consciously designed as an imitation of the centuries old, Holy Well. In many ways, this factory became a faithful copy of the original well that had freely supplied water for centuries through the processes of natural filtration. In addition, this enterprise brought the *Schweppes* operation closer to the railway, allowing for commercial, large-scale, national distribution of the luxuriously branded *Malvern Water*.

The brand became so popular it was granted royal warrants in both 1895 and 1911. Consequently, with sales booming amongst the wealthy, spring water drinking bourgeoisie, there was very little impetus to improve the quality of drinking water pumped from the dirtier wells of impoverished wage-earners. In fact, this succession of events likely paved the way for the culture of branded consumerism of the 20th Century, whereby the underlying ideology of such products would begin to define our lives.

The growing reach and influence of pre-global industries can be seen in the way *Schweppes* co-opted this 'pure water' from a source of agrarian society with the sole intention of creating 'a successful imitation of the natural spring'. Doing so would inevitably diminish the significance of the original Holy Well, condemning it to the amnestic dust of history, whereby the company's imitation would eventually take pride of place in the mediated, heavily propagandised, modern perspective. Even if the natural fissures of the Malvern Hills were to run dry, *Schweppes* could effectively bottle tap water at its factory base, producing a marketable 'product' at the same level of prestige. That being said, *Malvern Water* – 'bottled-at-source' – now differed from water drawn from the Neolithic wells of Paphos, or the functional timber constructions of the Greater Leipzig region. This beverage, with a successful campaign of marketing and production, had developed beyond its 'use-value', and had entered into the realms of 'sign-value', as associated with the Baudrillardian perspective of consumption.

The *'Stanford Encyclopedia of Philosophy'* provides a useful point of entry for those unfamiliar with Jean Baudrillard's thinking on the topics of production, consumption – and later – his ground-breaking relations we now associate with his ideas on 'the order of the hyperreal'. This analysis of Britain's water production, and the actualization of an imitation water beverage, supports Baudrillard's early thesis that 'the transition from the earlier stage of competitive market capitalism to the stage of monopoly capitalism required increased attention to demand management,' whereby companies could 'steer' and 'augment' consumption; an era Baudrillard thought to have occurred from between the 1920s to the 1960s. The '*Stanford Encyclopedia of Philosophy*' continues; 'commodities are not merely to be characterized by use-value and exchange value, as in Marx's theory of the commodity, but sign-value — the expression and mark of style, prestige, luxury, power, and so on — becomes an increasingly important part of the commodity and consumption.'

For Baudrillard, our current paradigm is now structured around the consumption of commodities that symbolise ideas of prestige and/or identity. Consequently, these commodities correlate with an individual's standing within the realm of sign-value, and by extension, society itself. Sign-value requires participants to be conditioned, predominantly through the prevalence of advertisement and the societal tools of mediation (television, etc) to see beyond the material use-value of a product. It is to live, as speculative fiction writer, William Gibson suggests of the realm of computer networks, in a state of 'mass consensual hallucinations' whereby technologies have driven the impetus of amoral innovation.

Only through an acknowledgement of these perpetual, orgasmic hallucinations, can we begin to imagine how a vital resource (that once flowed freely at the rate of gallons per minute), now bottled in glass and plastic, and imbued with some abstract, imitative attributions, could result in the establishment of a multi-million-dollar corporation; despite the ongoing, environmental destructivity of plastic and waste, a system sustained through the backdoors of our apathetic complacency; our desire for products in a delirious game of signs and signifiers.

Through the lens of this perspective, we can begin to unpack the ideological significance of a product like *Malvern Water*, starting with an obvious concern for its physical tangibility; that is, it's material existence. *Malvern Water* is the naturally occurring liquid (water), initially encased inside glass containers of various sizes. In *'The System of Objects'*, published by Jean Baudrillard in 1968, we can find an analysis of this material operating with a 'universal function'. On page 41, Baudrillard writes: 'Advertising calls it 'the material of the future' - a future which, as we all know, will itself be 'transparent'. […] Whether as packaging, window or partition, glass is the basis of a transparency without transition: we see, but cannot touch.' For Baudrillard, glass 'implies a symbolism of access' whereby 'nothing but the sign of its content' emerges. He uses the example of the 'transparency of jars containing food products' offering a 'formal satisfaction', despite the relationship to the consumer as ultimately 'one of exclusion' by which the product exists as a metaphysical, unobtainable space. He concludes with 'glass's cardinal virtue,' [its] moral order: its purity, reliability and objectivity, along with all those connotations of hygiene and prophylaxis which make it truly the material of the future...' From this analysis we might see how water as an imitation of the natural spring, once combined with the 'cardinal virtues' of glass, produces a marketable product that becomes highly desirable in an age of cholera and dysentery.

Compare this analysis of glass with that of Baudrillard's analysis of natural wood, from which we can apply to the water well constructions of Greater Leipzig. He writes; 'Wood draws its substance from the earth, it lives and breathes and 'labours'. […] Time is embedded in its very fibres, which makes it the perfect container, because every content is something we want to rescue from time.' This particular analysis is fascinating as it echoes the processes of dendrochronology, from which we can age the wells of the Neolithic. However, Baudrillard rejects the simplistic 'dreaming of the ideal warm and human substance of the objects of former times' acknowledging their acceleration towards abstractive qualities. Whilst 'substitutes for virtually all organic and natural materials have been found in the shape of plastic and polymorphous substances' there's an acquiescence for the loss of 'symbolic naturalness' with new-age materials 'achieving a higher degree of abstractness which makes possible a universal play of associations among materials[.]' This paradigm is observable through a 'transcendence of the formal antithesis between natural and artificial materials.' Imagine, for example, those ancient, lacquered, tree-roots augmented with glass surfaces, operating as coffee tables; a fanciful talking piece for every living-room experience. Or, perhaps, the technological augmentation of our own natural bodies. Baudrillard concludes: 'These materials, though disparate in themselves, are nevertheless homogeneous as cultural signs, and thus susceptible of organization into a coherent system. Their abstractness makes it possible to combine them at will.' With technological advances aside, this analysis would adequately explain the movement of the bottling industry's use of glass towards plastic-based products, as the cardinal virtues of the former merged with the greater flexibility of the latter. The equivocal use of the term flexibility should be taken as deliberately ambiguous here. Whilst the physical attributes of plastic differ in a greater flexibility than glass, its production costs and manufacturing needs are increasingly tractable. This makes plastic an entirely flexible material, both in its ideological attributions, and its physical malleability, allowing for a wider variety of easy-to-produce, aesthetic designs.

A second, strikingly relevant example of this move towards abstraction can be found in *Schweppes*' use of local materials when designing their factory as to be in keeping with the atmosphere of the centuries old, Holy Well. Once again, the abstract significance of materials was used to generate the required simulation. As Baudrillard suggests, 'the entire modern environment is thus transposed onto the level of a sign system' whilst 'the traditional environment, for all its directness, was an environment of moral obsession that bespoke the material difficulty of living.'

A similar story of water production can be found in a small commune of the French Republic. Created from the province of Languedoc, (originally settled by the Ancient Romans looking for suitable drinking water,) Gard forms one of the many administrative divisions of France. In a small estate of Gard, named Vergèze, lies the natural spring, originally known as Les Bouillens. A serious, commercial, bottling enterprise began in 1863, until company setbacks ceased all operations twenty years later. At around the same time *Schweppes* entered into a contract with the Ballard family, the current landowner of the Les Bouillens leased the spring to

Louis Perrier, who later purchased the land in 1898. Around the turn of the century, Louis Perrier, an elected councillor and doctor of Vergèze, befriended the Englishman, St John Harmsworth, the younger brother of Alfred Harmsworth® (Lord Rothermere), the founder of the hugely successful, *Daily Mail*.

Louis Perrier later sold the estate to St John Harmsworth, who revitalized the production of drinking water at the site. It is implied, through 'the official history' of the *Perrier* brand, that St John Harmsworth renamed the spring to honour his friend and business associate. However, *Perrier* was advertised, predominately by the *Daily Mail*, as the 'champagne of mineral water', and through this guileful renaming, Harmsworth assimilated the prestigious sign-associations of both the champagne houses, *Laurent-Perrier* and *Perrier-Jouët*. To affirm the connotations of bourgeois luxury, Harmsworth used his imperialist connections, promoting his beverage amongst the colonial armies of the British Empire, and later, at Buckingham Palace, where his water was served to the Queen of England.

This reliance on the system of signs became vital for bottled water companies to survive the technological advances of the 20th century, especially when water chlorination came into widespread use. However, technological advances also exacerbated the products of mass consumption. Much like the *Schweppes* bottling factory, the *Perrier* plant was connected to the railroad in 1908, allowing for the international distribution of 'the five million bottles produced annually.' By 1933, that production rate would increase to nineteen million bottles. Large-scale production would only cease when an occupation force took control of the spring. Following the allied defeat of Nazi Germany, a young Parisian named Gustave Leven would purchase the bottle works from Harmsworth's heirs; and with his business associate, Jean Davray, continue to develop the brand further.

Through purchasing the latest in American machinery, Leven and Davray were able to increase water output to a record-breaking one-hundred and fifty million bottles in 1952. Achieved through the ambitious construction of an enormous building given the befitting appellation, 'The Cathedral', this visionary undertaking propelled the *Perrier* brand to new spiritual heights, matching the fever pitch of capitalist Americana.

Through this journey, we can see how a product like *Perrier Spring Water* develops into a product of pure connotation, and by extension, we observe the perennial death of 'a totally functional world', as Baudrillard suggests. On page 57 of *'The System of Objects'*, he writes: 'Something is revived here [in consumerism] of the ancient habit, prevalent in a world of magic, of inferring reality from signs.' The mysticism of the product – a Holy water, in this case – with all its abstract significance is transposed onto the communion of the production line, into the great naming of 'The Cathedral', operating as the genesis of its sign. This is an industry of cultural simulation built upon an object of the natural world where liquid water is captured at the occurrence of its source. Baudrillard continues, 'What emerges from the realm of signs is a nature continuously dominated, an abstract, worked-upon nature, rescued from time and anxiety, which the sign is constantly converting into culture.' This analysis unpacks the industrialisation and consequent sign-significance of spring water from both the range of Malvern Hills and the permeable fissures of Vergèze, particularly in relation to their natural presence. On page 64, Baudrillard concludes, 'The always transcended presence of Nature [...] is what confers on this system its validity as a cultural model[.] But at the same time the always denied presence of Nature makes the system into a system of disavowal, lack, and camouflage[.]'

Remember; whilst glass offers the 'formal satisfaction' of transparency, it is actually a relationship of 'exclusion', much like the 'presence of Nature' in spring water becomes a relationship of the natural world's 'disavowal'. These contradictions are later sustained by the illusionary and bewildering nature of the product itself. Through the example of bottled water, we can observe the murkiness of this amalgamation process whereby the inherent contradictions of the abstractive components are blended to form a tangible whole; that is, the commodity itself.

This abstractive is restored to a level of sign-value comprehension by the relentlessness of advertisement, the societal tools of manipulation, and by the culture of the sign, from which a functional reality has been substituted. This culture of hyperreality is perpetuated by the sign-value of products and commodities in the constant, swirling noise of consumption.

One could speculate endlessly on whether or not Leven and Davray – the 20th Century owners of *Perrier Spring Water* – knew what they were doing when they erected a 'Cathedral' to machinery, implementing a production rate befit for global distribution. Did they understand the metaphysical implications of this enterprise, or was their concern located in this passive inevitability?

In 1954, *Perrier* acquired other water springs in the surrounding French region, securing a monopoly on the water beverage market on the European continent. This twenty-five-year master plan of acquisition and proliferation laid the groundwork for *Perrier* to assault the North American beverage markets. *Perrier*'s success across the Atlantic was largely, in part, due to the abstraction of bottled water as a status symbol under the order of Baudrillardian sign-values.

It would appear that the continued successes of the bottled water industry in the 21st Century actually stem from an ability to continuously absorb layers of abstraction – layers of symbolic auxiliary – augmenting a sign-value significance beyond mere societal prestige, elevating itself, ergo the consumer, with an additional sense of moral virtue.

As for finding a thematically relevant example of this augmentation process, we might analyse the UK-based water company, *Belu,* where we observe the ongoing success of this virtue-as-business-model in progress. Over the space of ten years, *WaterAid*'s income has risen from £1 million per annum in 1987, to £102 million as of 2018. This is likely the result of one-hundred percent of *Belu*'s profits going towards the operational funding of *WaterAid*, an organization now working in over thirty countries, initially set up by the UK water industry in 1981. *WaterAid*'s public figures revealed that seventy-two pence in every pound is spent on 'delivering services and making change happen' whilst one penny is spent on governance and twenty-seven pence on fundraising.

Espousing an attitude of good parameters, *WaterAid* claims that 'employee salaries are regularly benchmarked against other charitable organisations...' In 2018, the organization's

Chief Executive's salary was £121,319. '*The Office of National Statistics*' 2019 update for the UK's Average Salary states the average full-time salary is £36,611 and the average part-time salary is £12,495.

In 2014, the number of employees whose salary amounted to over £60,000 at *WaterAid* was fifteen. Those top fifteen employees paid themselves a combined amount of over one million pounds, (at a reserved estimate of £1,060,000). According to the official figures released by the organization in 2018, the number of employees whose salary amounted to over £60,000 had doubled to thirty-one employees. The top fifteen were now paying themselves a reserved estimate of £1,250,000, making that an increase of at least £190,000, over a four-year period. However, the combined salaries of those employees now making over £60,000 is estimated to be at over £2,260,000.

According to *WaterAid*'s own statistics, '£15 can give one-person access to safe water', yet the organisation has seen an increase of £1.2million, over a four-year period, on high paying salaries alone. Moreover, whilst *WaterAid* claims to be transparent, there is an obvious attempt in their annual reports to confuse comparisons through linguistic inconsistency, for example, the 2014 report states company salaries as 'emoluments', whilst the 2018 reports salaries as 'benefits'. The data regarding large salaries is obviously designed to be perplexing and impenetrable, with key information presented poorly amongst the glossy, alluring faces of *WaterAid*'s ambassadors.

This all conceals the fact that a global water shortage, in fact – all suffering – is beneficial to job creation, and profit-taking; a reality of late-capitalism that we cannot seem to face. The trendy idea that charities like *WaterAid* exist to help in the plight of others is one of entire simulation, where the global strategy is actually one of sustainability, not in water production, but in suffering.

In 2012's '*The Pervert's Guide to Ideology*', Slavoj Žižek provides a vital analysis, delivered against a thematically relevant backdrop; that is, a landscape reminiscent of a Baudrillardian 'desert of the real'. Here, against this poignant emptiness, Žižek reveals how, '…a commodity is never just a simple object that we buy and consume.' Rather, he continues, 'A commodity is an object full of theological, even metaphysical nasties. Its presence always reflects an invisible transcendence. […] We are not talking about objective, factual properties of a commodity, we are talking only here about that elusive surplus.'

For the consumer, a bottle of *Belu*'s water offers the allure of an increasingly abstract, virtual perspective, different to say, the lesser abstractions of significance provided by a bottle of *Perrier Spring Water*. This differentia represents a product which draws upon its significance as a charitable donation. Here, consumers base a purchase not only on a commodities association with societal prestige, but also, as a virtue which can now exhibit itself through the act of charity. Moreover, the entire allure of charity is one of a signified surplus; whereby an individual's surplus becomes a signifier of their success; 'look at this person who can afford such a generous donation, they must be wildly successful!' In essence, charity is giving to the poor and unfortunate, only to take something back in return; that is, in the form of what has been signified socially. In fact, charitable donations of anonymity represent the worst kind of narcissism as they exist entirely as a form of personal absolution; the masturbatory act of signifying to oneself.

Here, we will refer to Miguel F. Doria's 2006 white paper on water consumption: 'the Penn & Teller: Bullshit! show found that 75% of the public preferred tap to bottled waters in a blind test and then started to sell bottles of 'L'Eau du Robinet' (French for tap water) for $7 while recording the "victims" with a hidden camera…' It is disingenuous to assume those victims were buying tap water alone; rather, they were buying the abstraction, the surplus, the transcendence of tap water itself. This adequately explains the success of a brand like *Perrier*, whose metaphysical surplus pertains to the significance of its bourgeois aesthetic – its sign-value.

Perrier's sign-value did not alter throughout the late 20th Century, even when *Perrier* mineral water was found to be contaminated with benzene, a dangerous carcinogen. Whilst the company believed the contamination occurred during the packaging and distribution process, *Perrier* claimed that its spring remained unpolluted; a statement supported by the authority of the French Ministry of Health.

What's so fascinating about this contamination is how *Perrier* believed its massive recall across the American and global markets actually aided in its public image, generating an acquisition of additional abstractions. The official *Perrier* story, available online, states: 'In 1990, the benzene episode put a damper on *Perrier's* expansion. In France, the affair rallied *Perrier* fans behind the brand, while the company's worldwide bottle recall served only to improve its image with consumers.' Here, we can observe how the discovery of a cancer-causing agent actually increased the level of a brand's appeal; an acknowledgement of honesty and trustworthiness that is significant enough to be absorbed by the commodity. This absorption and the ability to reflect criticism, represents the true power of sign-value today, where any controversial perspective can be altered to fit the simulated reality.

The commercial water cooler, found in most workspace offices is the ideal allegory for today's consumerism. Two taps offering either hot or cold water, both fed from the same bottled source, using water collected from the same origins, contained within the same synthetic material that you would find in a *Coke* bottle. Here, the water cooler merely exists to reflect the ideological significance of the commercial vending machine with its glass-fronted promotion of exclusionary, sugary delights. The existence of objects and commodities are inherently structured to be ideologically referential to one another, proliferating a virtual reality of sign-value significance.

The final step in Baudrillard's thesis is one of hyperreality, whereby we see our day to day realities saturated by the proliferation and imitation of these illusionary signifiers; a world where water, a liquid over 2.6 billion years old, has become transcendent, metaphysical and virtual; in service to a system that is endlessly proliferated.

This Baudrillardian hyperreality is perfectly demonstratable through the last step of *Perrier*'s journey, where in 1992, *Nestlé* acquired the brand and its assets. Today, the Vergèze – a naturally occurring spring – 'produces 11 billion litres of water annually', under seventy-three different brand names, 'including *Perrier, Vittel, Valvert* and *Contrex*, as well as *Nestlé Pure Life* and *Nestlé Aquarel*.'

Every single one of these brand names offers to its consumers a slightly different perspective, a slightly alternative reality, whereby each consumer's needs, wants and desires are reflected by the commodity itself.

Here, each signifier – each bottle of water – relies on a differentia, a set of abstractions reflected by another, each beverage set neatly on the shelves of a chilling unit, set behind a glass door, tossed into a gym bag, displayed on a table for everyone to see – a relationship of illusionary significance endlessly proliferated by our commodities.

This is the world we occupy today.

A Suspension of Disbelief

On the 11th December 2003, somewhere in a bookish part of London, sitting against a backdrop of glass-fronted shelving units, Slavoj Žižek delivers a lecture on 'The Reality of the Virtual.' Just short of a decade later, the same lecture is uploaded to a YouTube account where it amasses over one-hundred-thousand views.

Here, Žižek states:

"...if somebody asks you 'do you really believe in Santa Claus, Christmas?' You would say, 'No – I just pretend, because of the children, it's not to disappoint them', but then we know how the game goes on and on. If you ask the children, they say, 'No, we just play that we are naïve not to disappoint our parents and to make sure that we get the presents' and so on and so on – but it's not only with children; it's even with our political life, I'm tempted to claim. Now, in our so-called - wrongly so-called, I claim – because we believe more than ever in our so-called cynical era, for example, I don't think anyone believes in democracy, but nonetheless we want to maintain appearances. That is to say, there is some purely virtual entity whom we do not want to disappoint. Who has to be kept innocent – ignorant, because of who we have to pretend; so, the paradox is that although nobody effectively believes – it is enough that everybody presupposes someone else to believe, and the belief is actual, it structures reality, it functions."

I sometimes wonder if this presupposed belief in democracy actually requires an additional 'suspension of disbelief' at the failures of it. Democracy, in fact, all political life functions as a subsidiary of modern living, which is effectively an ability to suspend our disbelief in the face of its own hyperreal absurdity. We go to work, fraternize with people we dislike, dress according to the fashion, go home – cry – shield our genuine selves from the sanctimony and judgement of others, etc. In short, we operate with what Samuel Taylor Coleridge wrote as 'that willing suspension of disbelief for the moment, which constitutes poetic faith' – after all – we operate with an illustrative faith in the ongoing functionality of our everyday lives.

This is what makes disaster films so spectacularly horrific to us, I suspect, particularly Post-9/11, whereby we are disturbed – not by the suffering endured by other human beings – but rather the idea that life's functionality, its ease of operation, the day to day monotony of things, the material objects which we have worked tirelessly for, our property rights, etc, which is to say 'our suspension of disbelief' – would ultimately come to an end. A solar flare will cleanse the earth of all technological advances, plunging humanity into a new dark age of despair; but what is really sad to the average viewer, I think, is to imagine all of the house cats not being fed by their owners before work.

It is not our intricate understanding of particular objects, (television, computer, games console, etc.) that arouses us, but rather their ability to function without demanding too much attention to themselves, especially in regards to their means of operation. Think of it like this, objects sitting flat-screened, streamlined, designed to occupy less and less of our external space, whilst paradoxically occupying more of our inner lives, where we blindly accept the software update – the importance of finding the next conveniently located electrical socket. Afterall, we know when it is time to charge the iPad, the mobile phone, the gizmo, the gadget – everything else. Perhaps even knowledge itself is unnecessary – extracurricular – outsourced and delivered back to us as opinion polls, advertisements and formal consultation.

Beyond this, a knowledge of the intricate technological workings of these objects is completely absent, nonetheless their functionality is what sustains their presence in our homes. The smart phone, for example, is a truly revolutionary device, allowing portable functionality, allowing us to email our boss, watch pornography, or both. Even so, we have arrived at a period in time where our technology knows more about us, than we know about it. In a truly narcissistic manifestation – today – technology is perhaps the ideal romantic partner because it asks for nothing in return, other than to know who we really are.

Imagine this: a couple sitting across from me, both on their mobile handsets, enjoying separate, virtual worlds in a Mexican restaurant that claims to sell Mexican food – activities that surely require some suspension of disbelief; another willingness to suspend our critical faculties and believe something surreal.

Surreal – that not only would someone like that be invited for dinner, but they could do it in Mexico, whilst enjoying the orgasmic spectacle of information – of cat videos and the like – being beamed straight across their retinas, all in the comfort of their designer skinny jeans. This is what it means to observe surrealism in the 21st Century, to feel as if you must be dreaming.

Taste the Feeling (or, I'm really behind on my domestic terrorism/ bombing campaign.)

I'm finding something,

the antonym of every slogan.

This is how a human being stands in motion

with a can of Coca-Cola

tasting the feeling.

A bland intoxicant, mournful in cacophony

with the indifference of no hushing up.

It is unreasonable for rail passengers

to plead for the same legal protection

as farm animals.

At this point,

horrible and weary.

Adventures in Hyperreality

A train ticket to the modern city is the admission fee to the order of the hyperreal. It is the material gateway to a distorted sense of reality and illusion. Exiting a train at Manchester Piccadilly, for example, and you begin across a grey gangplank towards the hypnotic lights of *Upper Crust, Yo!Sushi* and an *M&S Simply Food*. These spheres of convenience are peppered with neon and billboard aiming to please and prime, psychologically, each and every arriving consumer.

Navigating this world of hypnotic images is easy for the indoctrinated, that is with the exception of a singular peculiarity appearing saturated with a less than an obvious intent. Spilling forth from Manchester's train station brings out an image that stands with the warped sentimentalism of monumental propaganda. This is *'Victory Over Blindness'*; a statue depicting seven blinded soldiers from the First World War. In the endless recycling of war imagery, we are left with an unusual banality of expression. That is to remove all meaning from the actual suffering undertaken and deliver in its place the facelessness, cold bronze of some distant mythology. True poignancy could be achieved, for example, through the rendition of those maimed during the Manchester bombing of 2017 – a reminder of disastrous foreign policy and the crippling austerity measures of the here and now. However, the real message of these blind soldiers isn't to jog our blind memory from our blind ignorance, but rather to remind commuters that no matter how hellish the landscape will appear here on out, it will never be as hellish as the mythologized iconography of the past, which is to continuously address a bygone unchangeability as opposed to the cruel reality of our everyday lives as they appear today. In *'Victory Over Blindness'*, the horrors of the past are used to hide the new horrors of the present, and in doing so conceal the horrors of the future.

Of course, reminders of the 2017 bombing are everywhere in the safely-coded iconography of the yellow/black bumble bee, an image no more regulated than at Manchester's independent retailer of the year. Approaching this 'totem of indie commerce', the swollen, bloated masses are greeted with no fewer than three *Café Nero* and no fewer than twice that many homeless faces. In 2018, *The Manchester Evening News* reported a sevenfold increase in homelessness since 2010, one of the highest figures for homelessness outside of London.

The harsh realities of homelessness are often used as evidence of the system's failures when on further consideration these everyday signifiers of poverty are integral to the overall system's success. The threat of homelessness amongst the order of the hyperreal becomes another continuous and visible deterrent for those who fail to play along with it. Charities that target homelessness and mental health issues, in particular, often focus primarily on the social reintegration of the individual with neoliberal economics profiteering from the symptomatic, rather than addressing any serious causation. In fact, many charities obviously rely on this continuous cycle of social disintegration to provide lucrative administration salaries (and expenses) to their managerial staff. Whilst *Oxfam*, for example, panhandle for donations across socioeconomically disadvantaged highstreets, CEO Mark Goldring claims £12,006 in expenses to supplement his £127,753 salary.

Affleck's Palace then, also described as an 'emporium of eclecticism', is four floors of independent boutiques and stalls that have (to everyone's great admiration) somehow managed to avoid the stringent demands of retail law. The proverbial fly in the anarcho-capitalism arrives on entrance, where the consumer is greeted with a flaccid mantra of anti-phobias, displayed through the visual hierarchy of a flight of stairs. This is all proceeded by a sign of instruction, ordering the clientele to report any 'hate crime' – as if the culprit of such reckless hatred already existed inside the building – or inside of us – waiting for an exorcism. These signs appear in a city that has seen a huge spike in violent crime, where serious investigation is derailed by backroom conversations of what is and isn't cost effective policing. Of course, illusions of eclecticism fade from memory, especially towards an exit, where the bumble bee iconography reappears, once again, in the form of broaches, anklets, necklaces, tee-shirts, and the other assorted co-opted manifest of consumer trash.

The tragedy of these symbols, in relation to sign-economy, are in their exploitation towards profits. Through these signs and ideological assurances, we are confronted, absorbed, gilded by our melancholic apathy for a system that offers the pretence of consideration and empathy, whilst obviously diminishing both. Let's compare, briefly, Manchester's independent retailer of the year to the department store, *Selfridges & Co*.

This is Manchester's 'glass-fronted department store for iconic, high-end fashion, beauty and electronic designer brands.' Whilst *Affleck's* presents an alternative (faux-rebellious) consumer experience, *Selfridges & Co*. presences the standardized, old-world consumerism of *Gucci, Chanel* and *Louis Vuitton*. In many ways, both department stores work in tandem with the other, peddling in the signs and signifiers of their conflicting worldviews. However, when you overlook those shop owners trying to earn a living through some increased level of self-determination, the only real difference between these two department stores is an aesthetic one.

In an attempt to escape these worlds of consumption, you would expect to walk around somewhere like *Manchester Art Gallery* and feel a certain level of cathartic rejuvenation. As of early 2019, *'Halima Cassell: Eclectica–global inspirations'* forms an intense illustration of the distillation of modern values as they appear under the order of the hyperreal. Cassell's exhibition includes 'the debut of her latest piece, *'Virtues of Unity'*, an assemblage of ceramic sculptures which when complete will represent every nation on earth.' Consequently, everything remains bleached, whitewashed, and sterile; representing a unified art of pure banality, where the co-opted and appropriated 'global techniques' of production – alienated and divorced from their local origins – become exalted and the human subject nullified by the neat, cold, calculated turns of perfect, mathematical geometry. The most fascinating aspect of the hanging pieces is in their lighting arrangement, the obscure shadows cast on the walls behind, presenting the spectre of some contorted, human ghost that might have existed somewhere, once upon a time, before the clumsy inter-connections of globalist bleaching. A return to the world of manufactured environments occurs as you rise through the other whitewashed floors of the art gallery, with each new world connected by the cold, industrial skeleton of glass elevators.

Somewhere in the middle-ground, relegated to a small, dim exhibition room (for reasons of preservation) sits, with the familiar, suffocating air of mythology, *'Leonardo da Vinci: A Life in Drawing.'* Whilst we can assume pragmatically, that the room is designed for preservation, the sepulchral atmosphere contemporaneously frames the works with a perverse and contemporary desire for the disintegration of human forms. Many of these works of art are sketches at best, faded and drawn to the foreground; diminishing in real-time. On further consideration, the spiritualism and grotesquery of these drawings, at least, remind us too clearly of our genuine-selves, and so the masses reappear from their entombment, appearing noticeably disappointed – unsatisfied – as if all great works of art are best enjoyed unseen. Evidently, these works of art cannot compete with the ecstasy of the modern world, and on exiting the exhibition, *'A Life in Drawing'* develops into a fascinating spectacle; like a great movement of people emerging, spilling forth from a dimly-lit cinema screen, wishing they hadn't wasted the money.

In fact, the cinematic (voyeuristic) lens of photography appears on the final floor of the gallery, featured in, *'Martin Parr: Return to Manchester.'* According to the bland, website copy, 'Martin Parr shows how the lives of Mancunians have changed but also reveals how there is continuity in how we live our lives.' Sean O'Hagan, reviewing for *The Guardian*, wrote that Parr's vision showed a world that was 'less commercial' a place that existed before 'corporate branding made our cities dully homogenous.' This hides the real concern that Parr's work aids the bourgeois normalization of industrial communities as crass and parochial. Afterall, these images offer an explicitly bourgeois world-view, where the working-class subject is often reduced to the lazy caricature of *Kwik Save* clientele. Moreover, it forms evidence number one to the widespread osmosis of fakery and playacting of late-20th Century Britain. Parr's subjects stand gleefully with larger-than-life smiles, clutching their eventual seafaring shopping bags of mass-consumption – the trolley carts of utility – and the children who would inherit a world of ever-accelerating integration between what's real and what isn't. That is to say hyperreality itself. To say Parr celebrates 'the humanity of the everyday' is to ignore the genuine concerns of our human disintegration behind the corporate signs of an apocalyptic neoliberalism. Nowhere is more bereft of this humanity than Manchester Cathedral, a performance space so devoid of its congregation, they must have fled for the cake shop next door.

And for their dinner, *TGI Friday's* is an enterprise that promises to finally dissolve the conceptual nature of the Gregorian calendar for the price of a two-for-one cocktail and meat (with or without bones) slathered with sugar molasses. The speedballs of the western world are enjoyed through the good feel vibes of one hit wonders and waitresses with almost-real names.

Tell me, What Exactly is the Function of a Rubber Duck?

A **northern powerhouse** like Manchester differs greatly in identity and atmosphere than that of a southern, plutocratic city like Oxford. The atmosphere of Oxford is the atmosphere of the end of history. Everyone is walking around, checking their timepiece in pathological agitation, wondering when it'll all just come to an end.

The abstraction of Oxford is concerned with its prowess as conveyed by an intellectual past. At a subconscious level, it's like everyone is exhausted by the pretence of the abstraction; an exhaustion finding representation in the tired faces of every disappointed tourist.

With the fetishization of this abstraction, the city fails to advance with the tangibility of a coherent present identity. Consequently, there arrives in its place a fascination with *'Harry Potter'*; the endless infantile perpetuation of a utopian ideal nobody actually received.

Most shops sell a crossover of Oxford University hoodies and *'Harry Potter'* merchandise making the contents of every tourist's shopping bag an amalgamation of soft garments and a plastic *Nimbus 2000*.

What's so fascinating about the character of *'Harry Potter'* is his personal geography, the noncommittal straddling of two simultaneously occurrent worlds; that is, the phantasmagorical world of magic and the material world of the muggle-born. Ironically, Harry's early life of domestic incarceration and mistreatment under the Dursley household is perhaps more perplexing to us – more unbelievable – than the world of wizardry which he later occupies.

Whilst we expect the world of magic to be both alien and dreamlike, it's actually a world made profoundly functional and pragmatic. Most spells move objects, open locks, repair broken, functional items like that of a pair of cracked spectacles. Moreover, for the wizarding world, functionality is paramount to a thing's existence; at one point, Arthur Weasley asks, 'Now Harry, you must know all about Muggles. Tell me, what exactly is the function of a rubber duck?'

What makes Harry Potter fascinating to the citizens of this magical world is his ambiguity; his lack of function. Afterall, Harry was targeted by a profoundly functional killing curse, and yet remains 'the boy who lived'. Much like the villain, Lord Voldemort, (whom wishes to demonstrate his resentment through the powers of destruction,) Harry's existence becomes another challenge to the system of witches and wizards; a challenge of incompatibility with the natural functions of their world. In fact, Harry's journey isn't really about defeating evil, but rather a journey of reconciliation with his own survival. Much like 'Harry Potter', we all live and survive despite the odds – despite our consciousness – our apparent incompatibility with life itself. In many ways, we're all mesmerized by this story of existential reconciliation.

Suppose, in some other novel or film, you had a story of reversals, where a child, born into this functional world of magic, is shown an alternative paradigm where everyone is enthralled by rubber ducks and motorcars? And yet, which of these two worlds would suddenly seem more alien, more bizarre?

What's distinctly utopian about Harry's universe isn't the magic, or the spectacle, but rather a distinct lack of reliance on electrical technologies appearing alongside the proliferation of old-world architecture and imagery. Even the Hogwarts Express becomes a steam-powered locomotive designed to fill readers and viewers with a heightened sense of imaginative nostalgia for a world many do not know or recognize. This sense of nostalgia, a longing for a simpler, functional (yet humanistic) approach, is the significant appeal of Harry's universe.

Mead is served in inns, Diagon Ally resembles the localized, tight-knit community of a cobblestoned, by-gone high street experience, (an antithesis to the sterility of megamalls and faceless, digital spaces,) and when the cosmopolitan, worlds-straddling Hermione orders a cappuccino in a London greasy spoon, Ron looks at her with a face of utter incomprehension. Afterall, he lacks that access to the global significance of a cup of coffee; Ron Weasley is restricted – local only to his world.

Oxford's ties with the production of the 'Harry Potter' franchise, exacerbated by the proliferation of old-world architecture and imagery gives the abstraction of that magical world a concrete tangibility, a physicality you can really touch. Tourists, students, and the fans of that world flock to see the reverence of The Christ Church Dining Hall, The Duke Humfrey's Library, The Divinity School, The Bodley Tower Staircase, The New College's Cloisters and Courtyard.

Like a new-age Jerusalem, pilgrims pay homage to the fiction, caught up in the religiosity of its idols and relics. From its dreaming spires, to the cobblestone streets, everything about Oxford City exalts the aesthetics of *The Hogwarts School of Witchcraft and Wizardry*; it is spectacularly simulated, and as Baudrillard writes in *'Simulations'*; 'The simulacrum is never that which conceals the truth – it is the truth which conceals that there is none.'

Technological Slavery

There's a wonderful line from the Anne Sexton poem, *'Rowing'*, where the speaker, presumably the author herself, states: 'and I know that that island will not be perfect, / it will have the flaws of life, / the absurdities of the dinner table…' Films like Verbinski's *'A Cure for Wellness'* break free from the endless cycle of an unvaried milieu; a contrast to a cinematic culture that values the faux-subversion of our prevailing ideologies. This is the true animus of difficult, usually bad, usually obstructive, films; where occupying an age of a reduction of human complexity, the average viewer leaves instinctively repulsed by a reflective mania; physically shaken from their states of observational passivity.

In many ways, 'bad films', those that find themselves universally panned, criticised and lauded as box-office failures, usually show us 'the absurdities of the dinner table…' in ways that make us feel more emotion than those films that might be considered a box-office success. This would explain the universal interest in a film like Tommy Wiseau's *'The Room'*, a strange film that can only be described as characteristically absurd, possessed by an uncanniness so intense that we can't help but feel intrigued. Tommy Wiseau's character shows us a plasticized manifestation of our professional identities, the play acting of the average, over-socialised Californian, exemplified by uncomfortable inanity, an obvious discontent with one's own skin.

The importance of watching bad films can also be found in a production like *'Ghost in the Shell'*, directed by Rupert

Sanders. This film, in particular, manages to frame an existential nihilism in a way that makes technological slavery seem like a desirable outcome. What's worse is how the film buried this atrocious philosophical proposition under the guise of a superficial controversy surrounding its production. In brief, countless articles were written about the apparent whitewashing of the film's casting, with the lead role given to a white woman rather than a Japanese actress, as social media deemed more appropriate. In fact, Japanese fans were left surprised by this outrage, with Sam Yoshiba, the director of the international business division at Kodansha's Tokyo headquarters saying, 'we never imagined it would be a Japanese actress in the first place.'

Countless more articles were written after the film's inevitable failure, with a particular focus given to the derivative nature of the film's story, themes, and general cyberpunk aesthetic. Adaptations, by their very essence, are always derivative. They derive the stories, characters and events from their source material. The only significant point of deviation from the original source material was in the philosophical search for the soul; a point of historic contention in Eastern and Western philosophy, with the material scientism of the latter suggesting that no such thing exists. It would make sense then, that a Hollywood adaptation would be less about searching for one's soul in a metaphysical sense but, instead, more about searching for one's individuality, memory, and origin.

This is, once again, to miss the point of the film. I sometimes wonder if the controversial production points of 'Ghost in the Shell' were deliberately accentuated to detract from its central proposition that humanity should either embrace technological slavery or die.

This is the choice Motoko Kusanagi, the main protagonist, ultimately has to make: either find her place in the neon emptiness of this brave new world or take a bullet to her chromatically-enhanced cranium. Within Rupert Sanders' adaptation, it's no matter of convenience that the big Hollywood reveal lies in how it was the brains of those who were against the techno-corporations – who wrote manifestos explicitly against technology – that were the first to be used in the illegal experiments that gave way to furthering the goal of technological transhumanism.

The message of the film is quite simple, then: we will come to use technology, even if it has to be forced upon us, as was the case with the industrial revolution, and the other technological advances of the past. In *'Technological Slavery'*, Theodore J. Kaczynski writes: 'The technophiles are taking us all on an utterly reckless ride into the unknown. Many people understand something of what technological progress is doing to us, yet take a passive attitude toward it because they think it is inevitable.'

Faux-States of Subversive Transgression

If you're anything of a meme connoisseur, you've likely heard the story of the doctor and the child. One variation reads something like this – A doctor must operate on a little girl. Unfortunately, she needs O-Blood. The hospital – understaffed and underfunded – doesn't have the necessary supply for a transfusion, but it appears her twin brother shares the same genetic disposition for the rare blood type. We gasp with relief.

The doctor explains to the younger brother that his decision will be a matter of life and death. He must give his blood to save his sister's life. Of course, the child sits quietly for a moment, pondering his existence, and then says goodbye to his parents. Following the transfusion, the brother asks, "So when will I die?" Through an act of miscommunication, the brother thought he was giving his life for his sisters. Thankfully, both children die on the way home in a fatal car accident.

While explaining the nuances of a joke is to squash any semblance of humour, an analysis of this particular vignette can be forwarded as the humour of dour subversion. Here, we have a twin brother with a Christ-like consideration for the implications of sacrifice. A story framed by a picturesque, naive, dare I say – clichéd – innocence where only subversion can deliver the unhappy reality of life. The children die, regardless. Subconsciously, I think we enjoy this story because the unseen tragedy is usually better than the happy ending. We adore dangerously compelling stories that invoke visions of hand-sheltered gasps trying to push the laughter back inside.

There's a reason subversion rhymes with perversion. According to the *'Cambridge Dictionary'*, subversion is about 'the act of trying to destroy or damage an established system or government. He was found guilty of subversion and imprisoned.'

It is widely thought that *'Game of Thrones'* was a television series almost exclusively about subversion, particularly in regards to the subversion of fantasy tropes. The damsel in the high tower is no longer guarded by a fire breathing reptilian, but rather wields the mythical dragon as a form of weaponized vengeance against the system that would seek to imprison her.

On inspection, this subversion isn't subversion at all, but rather the confirmation of an active hierarchical order where women have co-opted the patriarchal forms of oppression. Daenerys Targaryen – a woman – is now the commander of the slave-army, the mythical structures of power, and so on. Where is the subversion in Daenerys' turn to the tyrannical? Where is the subversion in Arya Stark sailing off into the sunset? Other than to mimic the sailing of Odysseus, the riding of John Wayne. The prevailing attitude of this show as a masterpiece of subversion is almost entirely wrong.

As of 2019, the CEO's of *Lockheed Martin, General Dynamics, Northrop Grumman* and the defence wing of *Boeing* are all women, making up four of the five biggest defense contractors in the United States. In a world where women have risen to prominence in the military-industrial complex, nothing about Daenerys Targaryen is subversive in the way it might have offered some sense of fantasy enablement.

Weapons are still being made, and children still die, regardless. This is the unhappy reality of life.

The unhappy reality of *'Game of Thrones'* provides a good representation of our flawed system where only an idiot would believe a woman is beyond corruption. This show is a cultural artefact overwhelmingly demonstrative of a prevailing status quo offered as a faux-state of subversive transgression – an endless summer, if you will – where we all enjoy the faux-subversive fantasy, before regressing to our faux-subversive reality. This kind of faux-subversion, prevalent in popular culture, operates as a reaffirmation of our basic principles. It doesn't matter who is in charge of the economy, our nation states, or the military-industrial complex, all that matters is the survival of the system itself. In simpler terms, *'Game of Thrones'* is not genuinely subversive, but rather representative. Its transgressions are illusionary, much like our morals.

We are at a point in the cultural and mediated landscape where a lack of perceived subversion is enough to be considered a subversive dynamic. Beginning its publication in early 2009, *'One Punch Man'* is a manga and animation series that plays on the nature of this strange paradigm. The protagonist Saitama represents the archetypal – sometimes reluctant – hero who can defeat any adversary in one punch. It plays on the trope of an undefeatable champion, satirizing the tropes of the heroic journey by using them in the most blatant, obvious ways. While the ease in which Saitama carries out his fight against evil is funny and entertaining, the message is often poignant; the damage that evil conducts is never entirely mitigated, even when faced with indomitable goodness. In many ways, *'One Punch Man'* deals with the emotional cost of an endless catharsis, where good always triumphs over evil, and mythic archetypes are never subverted. What makes this narrative amalgamation so comedic is the way it plays on the naivety of its readers and viewers. This was particularly evident when the second season began to premiere in April 2019.

Viewers questioned whether the show had a sense of longevity, they wondered if the story would get boring, or if the dynamic would eventually have to change. There was almost a complete naivety to the reality that *'One Punch Man'* was telling a story as old as time itself, where goodness always wins out over evil, usually with relative ease and very little sacrifice. (Much like *'Game of Thrones'*, this is considered subversive!) Whether it's HBO or Hollywood, this is usually the story we are given; and with ignorance for the circulatory mythologies of narrative, genuine subversion goes elsewhere.

It enters our real lives.

This is no longer the 1980s threat of 'Communist and Trotskyist subversion' forwarded by Professor Christopher Andrew in *'The Defence of the Realm'*, but rather the consumerist subversion of capital mediated through screens and billboards. This is a subversion that undermines the power and authority of the self-determined citizen, rather than the government; a subversion designed to lower morale, heighten anxiety and forward the rampant consumerism of our time where products that caused ecological disaster are reinvented continuously; rebranded, bought and sold as a new catastrophic negation.

Airports become a microcosm of our daily lives where we enter like cattle, become stripped of our dignity by machines and bureaucrats, and rewarded with a consumerist experience at the other end. (Note how the shopping experience almost always accompanies security checkpoints.) Forget mass-surveillance; if China ever wanted to get in line with Western subversion techniques, it would build a department store after the passport control at Tiananmen Square.

Collective Transformation

Stephen Fry's *'The Ode Less Travelled'* is perhaps one of the worst books ever written on the art of poetics. It should come as no surprise that customers who bought this item also bought *'The Penguin Rhyming Dictionary'*. Archaic, dishevelled, and likely rushed to the publishers, Fry's lengthy manifesto stands at an all-time winner on the list of awful things I've read at the library.

Unlike Fry, I do not have a problem with arbitrary line-breaks, lower-case, or any other contemporary poeticism. These things do not constitute a degradation of language. In fact, these literary techniques inform my own interests, awakened by poetry classes where I enjoyed, for perhaps the first time, both the content and the teacher, who I knew, even then, must've been overqualified, over-worked and under-paid. In the great industrial machine of public education, reading poetry was the first time I was genuinely encouraged to look for something deeper.

The one thing that struck me about this process was its difficulty, how each poem contained surface elements that gave way to an unseen depth that begged to be sought after. Until those poetry classes, words had always been used to convey a casual simplicity, usually in the form of a message, or a slogan; a marketing tool used to convey a piece of information. Of course, these messages were always imbued with a similar emptiness. It was always about the unbeatable taste of the *Big Mac*, or the way some toothpaste really could make your teeth whiter.

There's an essay written by one of Philip Levine's former students, called *'How Difficult It Is to Live.'* The essay, written by Mark Levine, now an associate professor of poetry at the University of Iowa, speaks about taking a class with Philip Levine back in 1985; first meeting the poet three days after Ronald Reagan's second inaugural. According to the essay, Philip Levine really 'believed poetry was the most important thing a person could do, and that poems bore the impulse for collective transformation without which lies and injustice would prevail [...] [Levine] spoke of the crimes that politicians and capitalists had done to language. The right words mattered, he said, because poems could restore meaning to language.'

One argument forwarded for the defence of Rupi Kaur's *'Milk and Honey'* is that it offers a point of entry for people who would otherwise not read poetry. This initiates a dangerous route that suggests good poetry should not necessarily be conscious in its complexity or rigour. That being said, beware the people who claim poetry should be entirely uncomplicated; they attack meaningful complexity because they are incapable of it. They hate what they can't immediately understand.

This leaves one with the initial conclusion that nothing about Rupi Kaur's *'Milk and Honey'* restores meaning to language. In reality, discussing love, femininity, and other revolutions of the week makes *'Milk and Honey'* less about meaningful complexity and more about packaging marketable issues to a naïve pseudo-intellectualism. It is the continuation of language that masquerades as meaningful; the quintessential manifestation of a bohemian creativity obsessed with the capitalist ideals of ambition and worldly success. If you genuinely feel represented by the poetry of *'Milk and Honey'* it's because you are shallow, and superficial, and you believe your life can be encapsulated by an *Instagram* post.

In a world of self-promotion, social media fame, and the marketable objects of ideology, it's no wonder a collection like *'Milk and Honey'* sits comfortably as a *#1 New York Times* bestseller. Don't get me wrong, I think *USA Today* were right to call Rupi Kaur the voice of her generation; cliché ridden, vapid, solipsistic. For a generation raised on convenience and television, this brand of poetry offers a pretentiousness to hide the nihilism.

In his essay *'Politics and the English Language'*, George Orwell begins with an analysis of language itself: 'Our civilization is decadent and our language — so the argument runs — must inevitably share in the general collapse.' Orwell was right to say this decline of language has both political and economic causes, and in our desperation for convenience, and the ease of understanding, we rush toward the precipice.

A Giant Peach

'The war, along with the fake and presumptive warriors, generals, experts and television presenters we see speculating about it all through the day, watches itself in a mirror: am I pretty enough, am I operational enough, am I spectacular enough, am I sophisticated enough to make an entry onto the historical stage?' In many ways, Baudrillard's deconstruction of the Gulf war in his 1991 text, '*The Gulf War did not Take Place*', mirrors the political events of the last few years, particularly in regards to, say, the removal of Donald Trump from office, which we can say, with almost some degree of certainty, will not happen.

Here, Baudrillard writes, 'The media promote the war, the war promotes the media, and advertising competes with the war.' The impeachment, in fact, the entire animus of Donald Trump, is about the people's 'will to spectacle', which has become the defining feature of public consensus. For Baudrillard, '…information loses itself in a completely unreal space, finally furnishing the images of pure, useless, instantaneous television where its primordial function irrupts, namely that of filling a vacuum, blocking up the screen hole through which escapes the substance of events.'

Representative, Tulsi Gabbard, a Democrat and 2020 presidential candidate, broke the party-line by voting neither for or against the two articles of impeachment facing Donald Trump. Before the Mandela Effect took place, I vaguely remembered Tulsi describing the events of impeachment as theatrical. Ironically, Gabbard's decision ultimately heightened the spectacle of the impeachment, proliferating the drama of the moment. In many ways, Tulsi Gabbard became a supporting role, a player rich with oratory skills reminiscent of Shakespearean majesty – I'm thinking specifically to her calling Hilary Clinton, 'the queen of warmongers… personification of the rot that has sickened the Democratic Party for so long.'

It was, however, Devin Nunes, a Republican member of the U.S. House Intelligence Committee, who described the inquiry into President Donald Trump as a 'televised theatrical performance'. After the 'Russian Hoax' this was to become what he called the 'low-rent Ukrainian sequel.' What's fascinating about these events isn't necessarily the accusations, the outcome, or Gabbard's neutrality; what's really fascinating is how, on the same day, the United States Department of Agriculture removed Wakanda, the fictional home of *'Black Panther'*, from their list of free trade partners.

I first noticed this news in *The Guardian's* evening summary, nestled inconspicuously amongst more pressing information on the impeachment inquiry – bracketed with the words 'just for fun'. A separate article from *The Guardian* gave a broader explanation on the topic, stating how the 'fictional country' from the *Marvel* movies 'was used to test systems' and so on. Later that night, the *BBC* reported differently, quoting the remarks of an alleged 'USDA spokesperson' who had said 'the Kingdom of Wakanda was added to the list by accident…'

By the end of the week, the truth about the state of the fiction was ultimately neither truth nor fiction. Fascinatingly enough, even Francis Tseng, the New York-based software engineer who had first noticed Wakanda's listing on the agricultural tariff tracker was, himself, confused, telling the

Reuters news agency that he, at first, 'misremembered the country from the movie and got it confused with something else.' This was the manifestation of hyperreality in real-time – a fake country being used in real-world scenarios by virtual software with users and viewers unable to distinguish between mediated realities.

The fiction of Wakanda was designed in this instance to stand in relation to the reality of America. This 'just for fun' story of reality colliding with fantasy is supposed to juxtapose with the seriousness of Trump's impeachment when in fact, there is little difference, if any, between this 'televised theatrical performance' and the cinematic universe of *Marvel* comics as both serve as counterfeits to reality – as simulation.

Quite simply, the story of Wakanda's delisting from the USDA is presented as humorous to make us believe that the rest is serious, when in fact all of the mediated information, the spectacle of politics etc, is no longer real, but of the order of the hyperreal and of simulation. As Baudrillard concluded, 'It is no longer a question of a false representation of reality (ideology), but of concealing the fact that the real is no longer real…'

Simulated Imperfection

The best music makes me feel nostalgic for a world I've never actually experienced; a kind of fantasy-enablement. When it comes to mainstream music, if we are not fed a steady stream of pseudo-emotion, it seems the lyrics will instead refrain from reality with a series of ideological assurances regarding the high life as the ideal destination of the rich and famous.

At the same time, I think it was David Foster Wallace who suggested that real music could be used as an anesthetic against loneliness. Although we might keep trying, it seems genuinely pathetic to consider music as a cure to the problems of our 21st-century modernity. In fact, we seldom bother with these considerations anymore. Sex, drugs and rock 'n' roll is the slogan that encapsulates today's societal mentality, where music is used to forget the human condition, rather than face it. To add emphasis, let me refer to Slavoj Žižek's *'Trouble in Paradise'*. Here is a short paragraph referring to 2012's Gangnam Style:

"On 21 December 2012, [Gangnam Style] reached the magic number of one billion views – and since 21 December was the day when those who took seriously the predictions of the Mayan calendar were expecting the end of the world, one can say that the Ancient Mayas were right: the fact that a 'Gangnam Style' video gets a billion views effectively is the sign of the collapse of a civilization."

It is rare, I think, to find contemporary music that does not revel in self-satirical meaninglessness, but instead grasps an unfashionable sentimentality; the kind of feelings you might even describe as lonely or wistful. eevee is a beatmaker from the Netherlands, whose music is imbued with this kind of contemplative, forlorn, lofi sound. It is the music of dreamscape hypnagogia and rainy cities. A music so painfully pensive it might even inspire a sort of low-key transcendentalism.

Going into 2018, I asked eevee what she thought about this kind of interpretation. The loneliness in her music, she said, came from the 'things that happened in my past that I struggled with.' Discussing her process, she continued by saying, 'I make music on my mood, so sometimes it sounds a lil sad or melancholic.' Through our exchange, eevee acknowledged that 'a lot of people feel alone' and whilst the interpretation of sound was always different, we both agreed that music could be therapeutic in a society where epistemological loneliness was a fast-growing cultural phenomenon.

I have listened to eevee's music in the bath when I am hungover. Even at my quarter-life, I have the worst kind of hangovers, the kind where I can feel the serotonin draining from my body like oil from a car. Even the vivid cheerfulness of a yellow duck is not enough to stifle the disappointment I feel for the world. This is not to sound characteristically intense or self-indulgent, but to understand how this music can genuinely operate as an anesthetic against loneliness.

In our growing landscape of ideological uncertainty, lofi hiphop occupies a transitional space where experimentalism can inform a penetrating, dreamlike experience. To borrow a term from Žižek, in its purest sense, experimentalism can operate outside of a complete 'ideological container' making it a useful tool in the artistry of music.

Originating from Denmark, Axian promotes this kind of underground experimentation, where phantasmagorical sounds offer another fuck you to the corporate hegemony of music as a disseminated product, with beat tape communities pushing for a more liberated aesthetic. It's the sound of low fidelity meets hip-hop turntablism, a vision that breaks free from the editorial constraints of commercial saleability; where the dominant philosophies of our time inevitably end up at the back of the queue, and at the bottom of the playlist.

Even so, Axian worries that hip-hop has become an increasingly overlooked genre of music; going the way of once predominant musical genres like jazz and blues. It's an anxiety we both share, but an anxiety that feels reconciled nonetheless; especially when we consider these alternative movements blending hip-hop with low fidelity production.

Despite this, we both see the detrimental correlation between the music industry and its hazardous effects on emerging artists. Axian concluded this idea by saying, 'these days everything's gotta be fancy, and it's gotta be about money, drugs and sex to make it in the mainstream, and I think a lot of people are conforming to the belief that that's the way things should be.'

Axian believes this corporate philosophy of material hedonism has turned music away from what he calls, 'the language of feelings' – a statement that seems imbued with the Schopenhauerian sentiment for how music should be: a transcendental experience. At the same time, he locates his promotion of these underground artists within a growing 'revolution against over-polished music' where conformity is about creating 'products rather than music.'

In the essay, *'Music at Night'*, Aldous Huxley conveys the idea that music, at its most integral reduction, is the equivalent of some of humanity's 'most significant and most inexpressible experiences.' During our conversation, Axian expressed a similar notion, forwarding the idea that creating music is 'all about conveying your feelings or emotions into something tangible.' Whilst operating under the hegemony of 'money hungry labels' he sees the wider industry as largely formulaic, operating through an absence of creativity. This paradigm stands at the opposite end of an artistic vision based on the principles of conveyed experience, through which audiences can learn to understand the world and their place within it.

Somewhere in South East China, on the fifth floor of another apartment building sits one-hundred-yuan wireless speakers playing the creative output of Gustav Åhr, a soundscape occasionally nestled between five-second soundbites of advertisement revenue. Here, lies a little bit of confessional America broadcast almost exclusively for the citizens of floor five, or at the very least, the citizens on my side of the corridor, or at the very least, my neighbours, who speak with beautiful tonal inflections of Mandarin, but do not understand, I assume, a single word of Lil Peep.

Over the course of two months, my girlfriend and I have been examining the lyrical content of Lil Peep's cybography, discussing with a certain intellectual rigour, the hook on his track *'Gym Class'* with specific attention paid to the lyrics 'Playboy bunny though, shawty look like a pornstar, / I know she love me cause she fuck me in her sports car.'

Let's backtrack by saying we are living in the age of Nobel Prizes. I don't care that Bob Dylan won a Nobel Prize, but I think it's important to use something, (anything) as a platform for justifying this fight against the reduction of complexity.

Let's backtrack again by acknowledging my Gibsonesque use of language, more specifically the use of the term 'cybography' – a subtle portmanteau of the terms 'cyber' (Gibson af) and 'discography,' which is beginning to sound like something far too tangible for the ever exxxpanding postmodern trajectory. 'Discography' literally contains the word disc. On the other hand, the term 'cybography' adequately captures the way music is now disseminated, stored, and analysed in comment sections across the digital stratosphere. I sat down inside the simulacrum of the social (Twitter) to speak to eery, a lofi hiphop artist from Norway, whose current 'cybography' has inspired the piano covers and tutorial videos that pepper my *YouTube* recommended.

"Unfollow brand accounts that try to be relatable. I'll emotionally connect with a robot before I connect with someone's marketing team." This was the first time I'd heard eery talk about "the general sadnesses that come with social media" – the pseudo-empathetic strategies pushed onto us by a desperate corporate hegemony.

"I feel like characters like Wendy on Twitter, or Burger King's twitter – or all of these corporations running this strategy of making their mascot come to life – have almost taken a note out of Disney's book, in how you could go to Disney World and meet Mickey Mouse or whatever and talk to him as if he was a real person. It makes you connect with the brand on a personal level, and I don't feel like brands – who ultimately care nothing about you as a person – should have that space in our lives."

While forms of advertising have always existed to "manip-ulate people into buying shit", eery acknowledged how the "sadnesses" of our world had become far "more apparent now" addressing the importance of digital spaces as a "forum" to "express these things and relate to each other about them."

I asked eery how he got into making music. "I got into lofi hiphop one summer when I was painting my grandmother's backyard," spending lonely days "listening to artists like philo (eli filosov now, I think) and deadxbeat." These influ-ences fuelled self-determination to, as eery described, "make something like that on my own.

From digitally placed vinyl crackles to the faux warble of a 1950's transmission, this emergent genre, spread through forms of memetics and compositional hybridity, is quintes-sentially postmodern in the sense that it is almost exclusively made up of an honest simulation.

From my fifth-floor apartment, I find eery's compositions create an unusual sense of longing for something unspecified and out of reach. This melancholic desperation is accentuated through the subversive use of sampled soundbites that acknowledge a sense of impermanence to our current states of hyperreality.

"I do feel lonely and alienated a lot, I spent a year sitting alone in my room in my mom's house, just making music and not going outside because I didn't have any friends – as we had moved the year before to a new place. I would say that my music might have been influenced by that, but for the most part, I make beats, so it's more something to get lost in, and have fun with, and forget all about it."

This reflective honesty stands in stark contrast with the popular outcry of closed-source ideological assurances – the self-perpetuated promotion of a reduction of human complexity. Rather than heal our anxieties through moments of genuine catharsis, most contemporary trends in music – all media, perhaps – offer to supplement the masquerade of our unfulfilled natures by suggesting that we, ourselves, are actually tremendously happy, wealthy, and definitely not depressed.

Mainstream trends, failing to connect with the severe needs of the individual, produces a void that can only be fulfilled by a meaningful acknowledgement of our loneliness, our limerence and our dire need for something new. Like eery, Nietzsche wanted his melancholy to 'rest in the hiding place and abysses of perfection', which is why, Nietzsche said, 'he needed music.'

Through the artifice of marketing, we are caged inside false perspectives of ourselves as imperfect beings from which products can be used to repair our ever-accumulating deficiencies. Surely, lofi hiphop revels in a simulated imperfection, and in doing so, might allow us to acknowledge the simulated imperfections within ourselves.

Just Call It Poetry

To sing

my sign as a proposition.

That whereof we cannot speak,

thereof we must remain silent.

With all our inability to understand

to proliferate what we do understand

to proliferate what makes sense

and call it truth –

whatever that is.

I suppose whatever *that* is

will get us through

to the end.

To a stone

on a mound

of simple earth –

to a bathtub

to a battlefield

to the trench dug out

in every heart.

Yeah, sure,

someone's singing, Lord, kumbaya.

There's never enough of it, really,
no matter how many times
two people meet in a hotel room
and fuck and say I love you
and all that, proliferate themselves
and between all that, watch films
eat popcorn, shit, etc.

To say
it was enough
to follow people
holding hands.
To say
it was enough
for silence
to be broken
like bread.

To sing this sentence as a picture
as a piece of reality, rendered spectacularly.

To call it beautiful –
to call it poetry.

Why Disneyland?

Aaron Kent: The difference between Disneyland and Disneyworld is whether you can see outside of it whilst inside. So, while you're inside a Disneyland there are areas where you can see the 'real' world outside of the park, but in Disneyworld there aren't any areas where this is possible. With that in mind, would 'Living in Disneyworld' be a more appropriate title?

Alex Mazey: The title is inspired by Jean Baudrillard's critique of Disneyland. He writes, 'Disneyland is presented as imaginary in order to make us believe that the rest is real, when in fact all of Los Angeles and the America surrounding it are no longer real, but of the order of the hyperreal and of simulation.'

I make a parallel assessment towards the end of the book when I write, '...the story of Wakanda's delisting from the USDA is presented as humorous to make us believe that the rest is serious, when in fact all of the mediated information, the spectacle of politics etc, is no longer real, but of the order of the hyperreal and of simulation.' Through this analysis, we see how the ideological function of Disneyland can be transposed onto the virtual realms of elsewhere.

For Baudrillard, I think, it's significant that people inside Disneyland can see parts of the 'real' world outside of the park. It generates the required simulation – that those environments outside of the park are 'real', when perhaps, they aren't 'real' at all, but rather continuous vectors of hyperreality. This is why we are all, quite literally, 'Living in Disneyland', as the ideology at play in the physical, tangible 'land of Disney' actually exists wherever we may go.

In this way, the hyperreal becomes something totally inescapable.

Acknowledgements

Variations of some of these pieces first appeared at *publicpressure.org*.

The poem, *'Say It with Me'*, first appeared in the *Morning Star*.

The theory of hyperreality, developed over the course of Jean Baudrillard's lifework, provided the critical lens in which to examine the conditions of my own experience. I'd also like to extend that appreciation to the works of Slavoj Žižek, whose work is frequently referred to throughout this text.

Thanks are due to my wife, Wendy, who even puts up with my 'mall fever'*.

I would also like to thank my parents, sisters, and family.

I'd also like to thank those who agreed to the interviews that appear in this book.

* Mall fever is a term used by Rick Roderick in his eight-part lecture series on *'The Self Under Siege'* (1993). In the sixth lecture, *'The Disappearance of the Human'*, available online, Roderick states, '…I am a person who suffers from mall fever. Mall fever may be the last symptom preceding the death of what Foucault would call "the docile body".'

LAY OUT YOUR UNREST

www.ingramcontent.com/pod-product-compliance
Lightning Source LLC
Chambersburg PA
CBHW060037050426
42448CB00012B/3048